Counselor Connection

connecting parent-child-school

Counselor Connection
Text copyright 2014 Erainna Winnett
Cover Design Adorability Designs
Interior Layout Carii Lu Designs

All rights reserved including the right of reproduction in whole or in part. The purchaser may reproduce materials electronically, free and without special permission, for classroom or school use only. Reproduction of these materials for distribution to any person other than the purchaser or an entire school system is forbidden.

Library of Congress: Cataloging-in-Publication Data
Winnett, Erainna
Counselor Connection
1. Parent Communication—Education. 2. Parent and School Relationship—Education
3. Morals and Values—Education 4. Interpersonal Relations—Non-fiction

ISBN-13: 978-0692202814
ISBN-10: 0692202811

CounselingwithHEART.com

Printed in the United States of America
10 9 8 7 6 5 4 3 2 1

Table of Contents

Aggression in Relationships	1
Boosting Your Child's Confidence	2
Accepting When the Answer is NO	3
Children Who Steal	4
Teaching Citizenship to Children	5
Different Ways to Improve a Child's Self-Esteem	6
Effective Praise: How to Encourage Your Child	7
Focusing on Cooperation with Others	8
Helping a Child Overcome Shyness	9
Helping Children Better Communicate Their Feelings	10
How Children Cope with Bullying in Their Early Years	11
How Children Learn to Make Decisions	12
How Children Negotiate Friendships	13
How to Employ a Sense of Responsibility within Your Child	14
How to Help Children Handle Anger	15
Mediating Conflict Resolution with Children	16
How to Help Your Child Avoid Peer Pressure	17
How to Help Your Child to Succeed at Taking Tests	18
How to Teach Children to Effectively Focus on the Tasks at Hand	19
How Your Child Can Learn to Stand Up for Others	20

Table of Contents (continued)

Improving Motivation to Do Homework	21
Improving Your Child's Unique Study Skills	22
Increasing a Child's Likelihood to Respect Differences	23
Increasing Parental Involvement in School	24
Instilling Manners in Children	25
Instilling Perseverance in Children	26
How to Teach Your Child about Diversity in Others	27
Motivating Children	28
Overcoming School Phobias	29
Perfectionism in Children	30
The Responsibility a Child Has to Play Fairly	31
The Troubles with Friendship Triangles	32
Understanding Self-Esteem	33
When is it Okay for Children to Tattle?	34
When Teasing Turns into Bullying	35
When Worry Affects Your Child	36
Teaching Children How to Follow Directions and Listen Effectively	37
Teaching Your Child the Importance of Personal Space	38
Ten Ways to Involve Fathers in Their Children's Education	39
The Essential Skill of Self-Control	40

INTRODUCTION

Raising children is one of the most important roles anyone can play in society. After all, it is our children who are the future! The array of issues, challenges and opportunities in raising children are mind-boggling. It's enough to make any parent feel overwhelmed and sometimes downright frustrated. If you're feeling that way, please understand first that you are not alone! Anyone who has or is raising children has undoubtedly felt the same way as you at one time or another.

I put this collection of my Counselor Connection newsletters together because I kept hearing parents say over and over again, "I wish I had all the great information from your newsletters in one place that I could easily look at." Although it is written primarily for a parenting audience, many of my school counselor colleagues have also expressed interest in having easier access to this valuable information. Why? Because it is always helpful for school counselors to stay in touch with what parents are dealing with in raising their children. The tips, strategies and insights contained in these newsletters can help both parents and counselors work together in creating a wave of positive momentum in children's lives that will help them be as successful as they can be. That is my intention and my hope for all parents and counselors!

Whether it's boosting the self-esteem and confidence of children to succeed, sharpening their test-taking and study habits, or dealing with a wide range of problem behaviors that are bound to come up from time to time, the Counselor Connection newsletters I've gathered together in this volume will serve as a handy reference for all parents and counselors. Enjoy!

With all my best wishes for you and the children in your life,

Erainna Winnett, Ed. S.

Counselor Connection
connecting parent-child-school

Aggression in Relationships

Children have unique and complicated relationships with one another — they're able to argue and be friends again in the same day! Because children are prone to swift changes in mood and demeanor, it's important to address how your child handles aggressive situations. By learning to help influence your child's aggression in relationships, you'll be able to curb the likelihood of this aggression turning into something much more severe.

Expression of Feelings

Often, when children argue with friends or family either intensely or subtly, certain signs of aggression are more prominent than others. Pushing, shoving, name-calling, and demeaning are all ways children try to cope with a situation in which they feel threatened or exposed. It's healthy for children to act on their feelings, of course, but not when it gets to the point of expanded emotions. If you see your child acting aggressively with a sibling, friend, or family member, take your child aside and clearly establish the difference between right and wrong. Even if your child is hesitant to listen, consistency in your message is very important. When repeated enough times, the message will eventually sink in.

As a parent, it's your job to look for aggressive behaviors and intervene before aggression turns into violence.

Signs of Aggression

In situations where you're unable to see signs of aggression (such as days your children are at school), it's still equally as important to be aware of specific signs. If your child is overly emotional when they go to or come home from school, it may indicate that there are aggressive activities going on. Always keep in contact with teachers and those close to your child while you're away, as they may be able to provide insight into your child's behaviors. By tapping into multiple sources of information about your child, you'll be able to stay apprised of any situations that need to be addressed. If none come up, then you're probably doing a great job!

REMEMBER:

- *Keep your tone as positive as possible, even when addressing a problem behavior. Talking down to your child can potentially make the situation even worse. Always maintain an open and honest dialogue where you're making your child feel equal.*

- *Approach the topic carefully but without hesitation. If your child senses that you feel uncomfortable with the topic, they may not take it seriously.*

- *Encourage your child to always settle their matters with words, not violence.*

Boosting your Child's Confidence

Children's early years are essential to their cognitive and emotional development. As a parent, it's your job to guide your children down a path where they'll feel not only motivated to participate in activities and school, but also with enough confidence to help them succeed. Boosting your child's confidence works best when you maintain an overall context of encouragement and excitement about their activities.

Athletic Outlets

Sports are a great way for children to become involved with groups and teams. When they cooperate with others to achieve a common goal, they learn skills that will help them greatly as they mature into adulthood. With a team sport or group activity children can actively engage in (and, more importantly, enjoy), they'll be able to achieve things far greater than they ever thought imaginable. Also, by working toward goals together and creating incentives for your child to succeed, you'll help boost that confidence even more and create a safe space for them to branch out.

Healthy Communication

Self-confidence comes from children doing something they enjoy.

Healthy communication is also essential when it comes to helping guide your child toward a more proactive path. Listening to your child on a personal level regarding what they want to do and how they feel about their activities will help you understand the best way forward. For example, say your child is enrolled in soccer because you want them to be, but they would rather play hockey. Which sport do you think they would more likely to excel at?

Encouraging your Child

Another effective way to improve a child's confidence is to work alongside them and offer helpful hints and encouragement. This becomes even more important when your child is working up to an especially important event, such as a final tournament or championship game, recital or other performance.

REMEMBER:

- *Be open to communication and ask your children what they'd like to be doing.*
- *Always encourage rather than discourage.*
- *Set your own agenda aside to focus on what's right for your child.*
- *Be the parent you'd want to have.*

connecting parent-child-school

Accepting when the Answer is NO

No one likes to be told they can't do something. But while we may not like it, accepting "no" for an answer is often necessary. For this reason, children should be taught to accept "no" as an answer rather than always trying to get their own way.

Why Accepting "No" as an Answer is Important

Hearing "no" can be especially frustrating for children because sometimes they feel like the answer is always no. Even though you know that's not true, it can still feel that way to the child. It's important to both openly recognize and affirm those feelings in children because it's the reality of how they're feeling. This does not mean, however, that you should change your answer or allow the child to engage in endless whining. You can acknowledge how they're feeling while still firmly saying that the answer is "no."

There are many reasons parents may have to say "no" to their children. It could be a matter of finances where they can't afford to buy a treat or toy their child wants. It could also be a matter of safety if their child wants to do something the parents might consider dangerous or inappropriate for their age.

Learning to accept "no" as an answer isn't always easy, but it's a necessary skill that will stay with children and help them learn how to raise their own children someday.

Teaching Children to Accept "No"

When there are two parents involved in a child's life, it is especially important for them to be on the same page concerning when an answer is "no." Children can be very perceptive about picking up on such differences between the authority figures in their lives.

When one parent says "no," the other parent should back it up so their children don't have the opportunity to play one parent against the other to get their way. Another way to teach children to accept "no" is to ignore the bad behavior they exhibit when they don't get their way. Refrain from giving in just to keep a child from embarrassing you in public or making a scene.

REMEMBER:

- *Be consistent when saying "no" to a child.*
- *Back up the other parent when the answer is "no."*
- *Don't give in to poor behavior to avoid a scene or discomfort.*

Counselor Connection
connecting parent-child-school

Children Who Steal

If you're the parent of a child who has stolen something, you're probably wondering how this could have come about. After all, you've taught your child better than that and provided them with almost anything they have wanted and everything they have needed. In spite of all that, plenty of parents find themselves in the situation of having a child who steals not knowing what to do about it. There's no doubt that dealing with a child who steals is very frustrating, but the good news is that there's help and hope.

Why do Children Steal?

Believe it or not, it's normal for children to steal. In many cases, younger children really can't distinguish right from wrong — they simply see an item they want. But in children over 7 or 8 years old, stealing could indicate a more serious problem. By this age, children should be able to understand the basic difference between right and wrong, and why they shouldn't take something that doesn't belong to them. There are a number of problems that could cause a child to steal. An evaluation by a doctor can discover these problems and put you on the path to dealing with them.

Dealing with Stealing

When you're dealing with a child who steals, provide them with encouragement to do the right things in life and explain the troubles that can come with the wrong behavior. Sometimes, explaining the consequences of a child's actions can be all it takes to remedy the problem.

It's important not to lose your temper and to remain calm, even when it's difficult. Just remind yourself that you're the most important role model your children have. They learn from watching you, your reactions, and the ways you deal with situations.

REMEMBER:

- *Teach your child why it's wrong to take something that doesn't belong to them.*
- *Make it clear that this type of behavior won't be tolerated under any circumstances.*
- *Help your child relate emotionally to the situation at hand. Ask them how they would feel if someone took something they owned. This is a great way to teach empathy and help your child understand what's wrong with the behavior.*
- *Ensure the item that has been taken is returned to its rightful owner — with an apology.*
- *Refrain from excessive scolding or lecturing your child. When you go too far with those, they often have an opposite effect from what you intend.*

connecting parent-child-school

Teaching Citizenship to Children

It's important for parents and schools to teach children how to be good citizens and what that means. Parents' political affiliation doesn't matter, because good citizenship can be taught to children of any background.

Teaching Citizenship in School

Although it isn't the only place children can learn to be good citizens, school is where they spend most of their time throughout the year. Teachers can teach children good citizenship skills without mentioning politics or a political affiliation. In fact, it's important for teachers to refrain from mentioning those affiliations; it's up to children's parents whether they wish to teach their children about political parties and which one they support.

Good citizenship includes obeying laws made by the government, but it is much more that. Being a good citizen is also about behaving in such a manner that is socially and morally acceptable to most people. For small children, this may mean crossing the street using crosswalks. For older kids, this could mean not taking things that don't belong to them.

The best way parents can get involved in teaching their children good citizenship is to model the expected behavior.

How Parents Can Teach Citizenship

This can be as simple as putting garbage where it belongs rather than littering, treating strangers with respect, or taking their children with them when they vote. Children like to model their parents' behavior, so if they see their parents acting as good citizens, they'll want to follow suit.

Schools can teach children the basic tenets of citizenship, such as the names of the states and their capitals, about the different branches of government, and other academic topics regarding citizenship in the United States.

Becoming involved in the community is another good way for parents to teach their children good citizenship. Whether it's volunteering with a political party, a civic organization, or at their child's school, parents can show their children how participating in the community makes for good citizens. Parents can talk about their involvement with their children, show them how it's making a difference in the community, and take their children to events when possible.

REMEMBER:

- *Demonstrate good citizenship to your children.*
- *Help children learn about their country and its history.*
- *Teach children which behaviors are publicly acceptable and which are not.*

Counselor Connection
connecting parent-child-school

Different Ways to Improve a Child's Self-Esteem

Young children are very sensitive to their developing emotions, which change in different atmospheres, situations, and social circles. In order to adapt to these fast changes, it's important for you as a parent to develop good self-esteem habits. Not only will this help your children in their future, but it'll also make them feel more comfortable in these ever-changing situations.

Motivating Them to Achieve Goals

Children are under your direct influence as they grow and develop their own complex emotions. By involving them in sports and other activities where they have the opportunity to set themselves apart from others, you'll encourage them to succeed. By taking a proactive approach to their development in these programs you can increase the likelihood that they'll develop strong self-esteem, even when they aren't the star performers. Remember that it doesn't matter how well your child does in these activities — it's about how much they enjoy them. It's important that your child participate in a healthy way.

When considering how to approach the topic of self-esteem, parents should take a proactive and involved approach.

Being a Guiding Force for Self-Esteem Development

Look to find ways to reach out to your children through their goals and hobbies. Children are more likely to excel in things they truly enjoy, and this goes for schoolwork as well. By gently working side by side with your child on developing good habits and proper ways of treating others, you can encourage them to take an active approach to almost anything they do. Acting as a positive guide rather than a strict controller will also help them develop a sense of freedom and independence. If you feel that criticism is needed, keep it as constructive and positive as possible, focusing more on what they're doing well while at the same time pointing out areas for improvement.

REMEMBER:

- *Your child is always going to be developing and changing, and as a result you will need to maintain flexibility in your own efforts to guide them.*
- *Continuing to develop your methods and your child's unique sense of self-esteem will help improve their mental stability in the long term.*
- *Be a creative and open outlet for communication.*

connecting parent-child-school

Effective Praise: How to Encourage Your Child

Children who receive regular praise for their efforts in life are generally happier, better-rounded, and more successful academically. It's all about what you say, and taking the time to give your child this praise could make a world of difference in their behavior now and as they age.

How to Praise your Child

We are all more likely to remember the negative moments than the positive ones, so taking the time to give your child something positive is certainly beneficial in a number of ways. Praising your child for good behavior, such as doing well on a test or activity, can provide them a great deal of motivation and encouragement, helping them strive to do bigger and better things in the world. Take every opportunity you can to praise your child. It's hard to overdo it when it comes to authentic, sincere praise for good behavior.

There are many ways in which you can praise your child that don't take any time at all. Before you start, take the time to learn positive words you can use, as well as negative words to avoid. It may seem pretty simple, but what you can learn might very well surprise you. There's always room to learn and grow as a parent!

What to Say

There are many examples of positive praise you can use for children. Keep in mind your child's age when delivering praise, as well as their positive behaviors you're proud of. For example, if your child is sharing their toys with another child, you could say something like, "It's great that you're sharing with John!" Another example would be, "I appreciate how well-mannered and behaved you were at the market today." These are just some of the ways you can praise your child.

REMEMBER:

- *Always make eye contact with your child when offering them praise. This way, your child knows they have your attention and that you mean what you're saying.*
- *Ensure your entire statement is positive — don't add any "but..." at the end of it because that tends to cancel out the positive thing you just said!*
- *Try to find at least three instances each day in which you can praise your child.*
- *Public praise is always acceptable, and encouraged.*

connecting parent-child-school

Focusing on Cooperation with Others

Helping develop a child's teamwork skills and capabilities is crucial when it comes to their future. Cooperation is a necessary skill all children must have if they wish to succeed in working with others in their school and home environments. Without these skills, your child may be more likely to distance themselves from others, and be less cooperative at those moments when it's most needed. As a parent, you can help your children develop their cooperative skills with both adults and other children. If you feel your child isn't responding to your efforts, there are a variety of methods you can try.

Work on Teambuilding at Home

By making sure your child actively engages in chores, homework, and play time with their siblings or other people in the house, you'll ensure these behaviors naturally carry over into the school environment. If your child withdraws from these scenarios and doesn't want to work or play with anyone at home, this can indicate potential problems in school as well. Communicating effectively and staying firm in your stand for your child's cooperation will eventually help them see that being part of a team and working with others is both fun and rewarding. This can be especially difficult for shy children, but they'll take plenty of cues from you if you're persistent and consistent. Try different approaches of communication to see which ones work for you and your child.

Talk to Teachers about Your Child's Teamwork in School

Even though your child may be willing to work with others at home, this may be because they are in a much more comfortable atmosphere with people they have known their whole life. Make sure you speak to the teachers and adults your child is directly involved with in order to get a full sense and understanding of their behaviors. Teachers will generally be happy to recommend a few activities you can engage in that will improve their sense of teamwork and cooperation.

REMEMBER:

- *Encourage your child to participate in extracurricular activities that require teamwork. Just make sure these are things your child enjoys!*
- *Constantly employ teamwork initiatives at home, with both yourself and the rest of the family.*
- *Understand that sometimes it's all about your child's unique personality, so maintain flexibility in trying different approaches.*

Counselor Connection

connecting parent-child-school

Helping a Child Overcome Shyness

Do you have a shy child? Many children are not quite as outspoken as others. While there is nothing wrong with them, shy children often have a hard time in school and other social situations because they have a fear of talking to and/or meeting others. There are a lot of things you can do as a parent to help your child become less shy and more outgoing. Let's examine the topic a little more and learn how shyness affects your child, as well as what you may be able to do to help the situation.

Being Shy: Why it Affects children

Many things can cause a child to be shy. Some children are introverted and simply prefer to spend time alone. Other times, it's a feeling of not being like others that causes shyness to develop. Sometimes, it isn't fun being shy. It seems that every other child is out there having a great time, and your child is left behind. For the child, it can be frustrating as well. It could even be that the child is very emotional and sensitive to the world around them. No matter what is causing your child to be shy, there are many ways in which you can help them overcome such a situation and be more in tune to social environments and situations.

Helping Your Shy Child

Helping a shy child is something any parent can do. Most importantly, it's crucial to maintain a positive and encouraging attitude about their shyness.

Show them that you understand their worries and what they are going through. Attend parties, meetings, and other social gatherings that your child can also be a part of. Ensure you're also teaching them the basics of socializing with other people. There are a number of age-appropriate ways to do this.

REMEMBER:

- *Allow your child to adjust to situations as needed. Refrain from forcing them to talk or participate when they are fearful of doing so.*
- *Encourage your child to be involved with other people. Allow them to see you interacting positively with others as well.*
- *Give your child books and other age-appropriate reading materials that discuss shyness and how to overcome it.*
- *Accept your child as they are. Some of us are just less outspoken than others — and that's OK!*

connecting parent-child-school

Helping Children Better Communicate Their Feelings

For any developing child, communication with adults and other children may prove difficult at first. Although we all learn how to communicate our feelings over time, children need special attention and care in this process. Because their vocabularies and sense of self are expanding every day, it's important to help them down this particularly challenging path. Without guidance, a child can often feel helpless and be more prone to angry or frustrated outbursts. To instill communication and friendship between you and your child, there are a number of things you should consider first.

Keep Communication Positive

Parents can be a great source of encouragement for children. It can be a real challenge to always maintain positive communication! When children do something wrong, they're more likely to grow upset if you respond with anger or frustration. No child is born inherently bad-tempered or rebellious; they pick up on the behaviors and mannerisms of the people around them. To better understand this, consider this simple scenario: A child has drawn on the walls with a crayon. A parent who yells and grounds a child for this act of rebellion is more likely to see the action repeated because the parental reaction makes the child feel like their independence is limited.

These kinds of situations call for a gentle but firm explanation of what's appropriate and what's not. You may have to take the crayons away, making it clear that they can only have them if they can abide by the rules of only drawing on paper rather than the walls.

Sometimes, It's About Honesty

When you're open and willing to talk with your child on their level, they will be more likely to do the same with you. Children respond best to positive cues and encouragement, so keep that in mind when you're developing your child's unique communication skills.

REMEMBER:

- *Always remain calm and assertive when communicating with your child, even in stressful situations.*
- *Refrain from talking down to your child in any way that might make them feel belittling. Put yourself on their level (physically and mentally), and help them see the error of their ways.*
- *Losing your temper with a rarely solves any problems. Set a good example by being gentle and firm.*

connecting parent-child-school

How Children Cope with Bullying in Their Early Years

More than likely, you and many other parents were either victims of bullying in your developmental years. You may have even been a bully yourself. As a parent now, it's important that you understand exactly how your child will react to a bullying scenario and employ practices that can help them cope with the stress this will inevitably cause. To effectively go through the motions and make this possible, you must do your own research into the practices and methods being implemented at the school where your child is being bullied. Furthermore, you must help your child cope with the bullying in a healthy and positive way.

If You Feel Your Child Is a Victim of Bullying, Reach Out to the School

When your child complains about a certain group of kids or doesn't want to go to school, there may be an underlying reason they don't feel comfortable talking about. Children who tattle at school often fall under scrutiny by their peers, so they may endure bullying just to keep themselves afloat. Talk to teachers if you notice any visual or emotional cues that may lead you to believe your child is being bullied.

They will most likely be able to paint an accurate picture of the situation, but they won't always have the information you need. If you suspect your child is a victim, ask them directly while letting them know you'll keep the information to yourself unless it's serious.

Teach Your Child How to Respond in a Healthy Way

Because they may feel self-conscious speaking out about bullying, give your child a few tips they can take to school with them to avoid these types of behaviors from other children. Let them know they can always walk away if they feel uncomfortable, talk to teachers, or simply find a new group of friends. Many children will undergo bullying of some type during their young lives, so make sure to let your child know this, and that it's important to resist the urge to fight back.

REMEMBER:

- *By telling your child not to fight back against a bully, you teach them not to respond by doing the same that was done to them.*
- *Encourage your child to always communicate with trusted adults when they feel hurt.*
- *Talk with teachers and other parents about potentially harmful situations, if the need arises.*

Counselor Connection
connecting parent-child-school

How Children Learn to Make Decisions

Just like adults, children have a very complicated and intense range of emotions. However, unlike you, your child's sense of self is still developing. Because of this, they may have trouble making decisions, or may often make less than optimal choices. This is a natural process that children all around the world go through. As a parent, you can help make sure your child understands a good decision from a bad one. You must also make sure they can grasp when a decision feels wrong. By helping develop these crucial concepts early on, you can ensure your child will make healthy choices far into the future.

Children Take Examples from the People Around Them

When it comes to a child that is just developing their sense of self worth and independence, they will take examples from the people they are closest with to make decisions. This goes for their peers at school as well. When you make a decision, they will soak up that information like a sponge and may react the same way when faced with a similar scenario.

Present your child with a series of hypothetical situations as an exercise, asking them what decisions they would make in those scenarios. You'll be able to gauge your child's ability to distinguish right from wrong during this exercise, and plan ways to help them improve if needed. This may sound very involved, but what better way to ensure your child's future success than helping them in the early years?

Children Are More Likely to Go with What Feels Good

Just because they may take in your decisions as reference points, children generally make final decisions based on their own needs and wants. Because they are still developing, they may choose a negative option over a positive one because the negative one will have better immediate results for them. Consider this when you're trying to instill good decision-making practices.

REMEMBER:

- *Children are very self-motivated to do things that feel good. Keep this in mind when trying to teach them.*
- *The decisions they make may not always affect them, or their habits may change over time.*
- *Always be aware of how your child approaches a decision at home.*

Counselor Connection
connecting parent-child-school

How Children Negotiate Friendships

Children are constantly developing and changing. The way they interact with others and how their attitudes reflect on their behaviors will also change as they grow older. Friends are an important part of all children's beginning stages, and will shape the way they think for the rest of their lives. Although they may not be friends with the same people when they grow older, it's important to consider how children negotiate these initial friendships and what it means when they're unable to hold on to them. As a parent, it's important to understand how your child and their friends interact with one another, and what you can do to help a friendship that's not going well.

Really Get to Know Your Child's Friends

Get to know your children's friends — even (and especially) the ones you don't like. Maybe you are being overly critical of the boy next door who when he comes over and doesn't seem very clean. Then again, another friend of your child's who may be well mannered could end up being a negative influence on them. It's all a matter of perspective and unique circumstances, but being aware and interacting with your child's friends will help give you a better understanding of their social circles. Children pick and choose friends they can have an enjoyable time with, so take a step back and get the bigger picture before you jump in and try to influence things.

Respect Your Child's Personality

Remembering that children also interact differently is crucial as well. They are constantly fighting, laughing, and changing social circles as they grow older. Just because your child may be having a hard time finding good friends doesn't necessarily mean they are anti-social — it may just mean that they have a unique personality and want to find friends whom they can easily relate to. Far too often, parents take their child's lack of a social circle as a sign of reclusiveness. They then begin to worry, and constantly overthink how their child is behaving. Try to be circumspect and avoid jumping to conclusions based on worries that may or may not be true.

REMEMBER:

- *Just because they aren't brimming with friends doesn't mean your child is any less normal. They may just be unique, which is a good thing!*
- *Refrain from judging a child's friends based solely on their appearance.*
- *Always discuss problems between friends with your child.*

Counselor Connection

connecting parent-child-school

How to Encourage a Sense of Responsibility within Your Child

Responsibility is important for all children's developmental years. Not only will they carry these skills through the rest of their young lives, but the essence of responsibility will help them make key decisions and hold key positions later in life. Although it may sound complex, giving a child a sense of both independence and responsibility at home will help them through their schooling and extracurricular activities, and may also translate to better habits all around as they grow older. By following a few simple steps, you can ensure your child will develop good, responsible habits. These skills are essential to learn as a parent in order to pass them on to your child for their future success.

Give Them Larger-than-Life Tasks as well as Small Chores

Overloading your child may deter them from wanting to take on a position entailing responsibility. By giving them one large chore or task to preform along with a few smaller ones, you can help increase the likelihood that they will complete these chores more quickly as time goes on. You can also help develop their sense of independence by giving them a chore or job that they have always been interested in. A great example of this is when children see their parents washing a car and want to help. The activity is exciting and fresh to them, so they want to be involved. Give your child a more challenging role than usual when you're working on a task together, and responsibility will blossom all on its own.

Get Them a Pet, or Something Else They Will Want to Maintain

When your child truly wants a pet and has the opportunity to care for it every day, they will eventually develop a sense of responsibility and ownership. Pet ownership is a great way to develop responsible habits; reward your child for taking initiative when not asked.

REMEMBER:

- *Although a pet is a good example for handing responsibility to your child, other scenarios work just as well.*
- *The promise of something enjoyable after chores will help motivate your child to get through them more quickly and efficiently as long as you don't overdo it!*
- *Encourage your child to take on leadership roles in school or play in a gentle and positive way.*

connecting parent-child-school

How to Help Children Handle Anger

Anger is a common emotion for everyone. Whether we're dealing with an issue at home, work, or school, it's to be expected that you'll grow angry or frustrated from time to time. However, anger in children is another matter entirely. When a child is angry or upset about something, it can affect their mood for days. If they get angry enough, it could affect their personality and behaviors in the long term. To help them deal with the anger they are sure to face in their developmental years, there are several factors to consider.

Do Not Respond with Anger

When children grow angry or upset, their emotions feel like a flurry of mixed feelings. If your child lashes out at you for anything, refrain from responding in kind, as this sends them the wrong message. When your child is angry, it is better to be more passive, ensuring you constantly repeat your stance regarding the matter at hand. Even if their angry behavior doesn't fizzle right away, it will with time. Shouting at one another in anger rarely leads to a long-term solution and carries the risk of forming bad habits.

Be Supportive and Comforting

When your child is feeling angry at something other than yourself, there are many ways in which you can approach the situation to help them calm down. Sit down with them and speak at their eye-level, putting yourself in their shoes and staying open to whatever they have to say. Use comforting touches and hugs, reminding them that you're their parent and they can always approach you with the tough things. If you child is angry as the result of being the object of teasing or some other injustice, it won't help them if you get all worked up yourself. The best thing you can do is to be a source of comfort and calming energy to help them calm down.

REMEMBER:

- *Hold their hand and let them know everything is going to be all right. Love can go a long ways to making any situation better.*
- *Talk in an open way, and encourage your child to express their feelings.*
- *Refrain from responding to angry emotions and energy with the same. Be comforting and calm.*

Counselor Connection

connecting parent-child-school

Mediating Conflict Resolution with Children

Conflict can be a confusing and frustrating time for parents and children alike. As a parent, you can help make sure that conflicts are resolved efficiently and within a certain time frame to maintain good relationships. Conflict-resolution skills in children are also important for teamwork tasks at school, and in their extracurricular activities as well. By working on a mediation plan and helping your child resolve conflicts with both their siblings and peers, you'll be able to encourage them to develop a healthy sense of conflict resolution that will serve them well long into the future.

If Your Child has been in a Fight, Resolve it Quickly

Because children are so deeply effected by the words of their peers, serious arguments and fights are commonplace among them. Whether it was a trivial or a serious dispute, always remember that an open line of communication is a good route to take. Don't be overly angry, but don't be too subdued, either. Let your child know that their behavior was unacceptable, and that they must do anything they can to repair the damage they have caused. If they refuse to cooperate, then you might have to engage in a disciplinary action to get your message across clearly and firmly. This is where the real parenting comes in. Unless a child understands the gravity of conflict, they will never learn how to resolve it with their words, which are always better than fists.

Your stance on matters such as these, especially anytime the fighting has become serious, must be clear and firm while at the same time understanding and gentle.

Have a Family Meeting if the Problems Are Internal

If your children are having issues among each other (or with you), it is imperative that you keep the lines of communication open. Don't pick sides or, if the fight involves you, don't grow angry or frustrated at a child's opinion. Calmly explain to all parties involved that there are better ways to resolve these issues, and try to come to agreement among your family members.

REMEMBER:

- *Encourage your child to bring their feelings and disputes to you before they take any sort of action they may regret.*
- *Always try to have this discussion whenever a problem is persistent. Don't just grow frustrated because it continues to happen.*
- *Conflict resolution takes time to develop, so keep at it!*

Counselor Connection

connecting parent-child-school

How to Help Your Child Avoid Peer Pressure

Peer pressure is a very real thing in the lives of all children. When they are younger, peer pressure can come in very small doses – encouraging them to bully someone who is insecure, asking them to steal something for the sake of everyone else, or even persuading them to play a prank on someone who isn't expecting it. Although these things may seem trivial or may be things you don't often think about when you hear the term "peer pressure," they are very real. By allowing them and choosing not to talk to your child about the effects of peer pressure, you may inadvertently encourage behaviors that will translate into the teenage years, where it becomes even more difficult to deal with.

Your Child's Friends

Talking about how friends should behave is important in this scenario. Helping your child understand how they feel when someone else asks them to do something they don't feel comfortable with is the first step in establishing a conversation. Use the following example: If someone asks them to eat something they find disgusting, would they do it? Why? Try and make the conversation enjoyable, giving them hypothetical scenarios that will translate into real-life lessons and conversations. Because children are easily swayed, you need to hold a firm stance when it comes to peer pressure.

Avoiding Peer Pressure

Explaining how to avoid peer pressure in the first place is another important thing to do. When your child is put in a position that they aren't comfortable with, they are more likely to respond to the requests of others rather than listen to their own conscience. By letting them know that it's okay to say "no," you can help them take the first step towards awareness. Because these things are not always talked about at school, it's important to establish good behaviors from bad ones at home. Ask your child how they would feel if someone bullied them because someone else told them to. Their response should give you a good gauge for how they handle these situations in real time.

REMEMBER:

- *Treating your child as an equal is important in any sort of communication. Let them know that these situations can be hard to avoid, but that they choose to say no.*
- *Ask them if they have been peer pressured before, and when.*
- *Help children understand consequences through various hypothetical scenarios.*

Counselor Connection
connecting parent-child-school

How To Help Your Child Succeed at Taking Tests

Test taking can be stressful for both children and parents. Not only do you have to make sure your child is fully prepared for the content they'll face, but sometimes it also feels like you have to force them to study. For children, testing can be scary. Unless the test is on a subject in which they excel and/or are excited about, children may feel intimidated and are more likely to be unsuccessful. These are all bumps in the road of school and life, but effective study skills and habits can be developed with your child – and with enough of your own involvement, these skills will transition into adulthood.

Work with Your Child on Study Habits

In a comfortable atmosphere, like their bedroom, bring in a set of healthy study snacks and sit down with your child to go over the test material. Don't hold their hand while they figure things out, but be available if they get stuck or have any questions. As a parent, you can help your child develop good study skills early on. Just giving them the answers, however, doesn't help that process. Go through different scenarios and ways to solve questions and problems together, but let them figure out most of it on their own.

Make Sure Your Child Has a Plan in Place — and Offer Rewards

When it comes to motivating a child to develop good study habits and test-taking skills, go through a practice run. If your child isn't enthusiastic about this, offer a small reward at the end to encourage them to try their best. After the test is done, go through the answers one by one, letting your child know how they did. The more you go through this exercise with them, the more comfortable they will be in a test-taking situation.

REMEMBER:

- *Ask your child what about the test they don't feel comfortable with. Work through a practice test with them, and help them understand there's nothing to fear.*
- *Remind them that it's not the end of the world if they don't ace a test.*
- *Be supportive, but don't offer them all the answers. Allow them to figure things out on their own.*

connecting parent-child-school

How to Teach Children to Effectively Focus on the Tasks at Hand

Children often have wandering minds. They're so preoccupied with thoughts of friends, play, and activities that it can be hard to focus in school. An important step toward the start of a great day for your child is a healthy and nutritious breakfast. Not only will it help them stay focused throughout the day, but it will also provide them with the needed energy to succeed at tasks. If they are having trouble focusing at home, encourage them to develop good habits with honest communication and support. If they are still having trouble, here are some helpful ways to help develop their focusing skills, which will serve them well in the future.

It's Not Always About Their Lack of Effort

If you notice your child has been having significant problems with focusing on tasks, there may be an underlying problem of which you're not aware. It may seem extreme, but taking your child to the doctor and having them examined a couple of times a year is a great idea. Sometimes, cognitive development is slowed by outside circumstances, and by force-focusing your child, you may be ignoring something you didn't know was there. Some children discover that they are OCD, ADD or ADHD when they're very young through this kind of vigilance. Then a plan can be created to address the condition.

Encourage Them to Perform Tasks Quickly for Rewards

When a child has chores, they are going to complete them much more slowly if they can't see what's in it for them. Letting them outside to play after doing their homework or cleaning their room is a great motivator for helping them stay on task. If they do a quick or not very good job just to get to the reward, patiently explain that the reward is based on doing good work. In the beginning, your child may need a good deal of support from you in completing such chores, but over time you can back off until they are doing them on their own.

REMEMBER:

- *Rewards like more playtime will help motivate children to stay focused rather than go astray on tasks. These skills will eventually translate into school and later in life to the workplace.*
- *If you notice something odd, have your child checked out by your family doctor.*
- *These skills can take quite a while to develop, so be patient.*

Counselor Connection

connecting parent-child-school

How Your Child Can Learn to Stand Up for Others

Bullying is a persistent and growing problem in both North America and across the world. As different methods of bullying come to light (e.g., social media, other online means), there are more things to worry about. As a child, being isolated from your peers because of being different can be a very traumatic experience. If your child knows of someone who's being bullied but is doing nothing about it, teach the child about the many steps they can take to help their peer. More than likely, the reason they told you in the first place is because deep down inside they are uncomfortable with the situation as well.

Developing These Skills Will Help with Self Confidence

By teaching your child that bullying is wrong and encouraging them to stand up for people who can't or don't know how to or aren't brave enough stand up for themselves, you'll help them develop a sense of self-worth and independence in them. These admirable traits will carry on through many things they do. Many bullies will simply stop if someone stands up to them. Be sure your child understands that responding with the same treatment bullies dish out is never okay.

Practicing Different Situations at Home

Let's say your child has brought a bully to your attention, and you want to help them understand how to react if they don't like what that person is saying to someone else. Walk them through a typical bullying scenario and introduce different methods to deal with these situations. Walk them through these methods one by one, practicing them whenever you can.

REMEMBER:

- *Teach them to use the power of words, not fists, even if another child begins fighting with them physically.*
- *If they feel physically threatened or are being physically abused, tell them to get away and find a trusted adult to help.*
- *Ask them how they would feel if no one stuck up for them in a similar situation.*

Counselor Connection

connecting parent-child-school

Improving Motivation to Do Homework

Homework can be the bane of a young child's existence. Most of the time, children want to be outside playing with friends or doing other activities they enjoy. Because school can be stressful for a child, coming home is like the end of a workday for an adult. Children simply want to unwind and be a part of a family experience, or do things they enjoy. However, just because they don't enjoy doing homework doesn't mean they can't get through it successfully. By making homework fun as a parent, you'll be able to encourage and help build homework habits for the future, ensuring your child is getting the most from their education.

Show that You Care

The reason homework may feel like such a chore to many children is that they find no enjoyment or fulfillment from doing it. Also, when they're doing their homework, they're probably doing it alone. By actively taking an interest in the work your child is doing (e.g., assisting them with any problems or frustrations they have), you have the great opportunity to make it a fun experience. It's unrealistic to expect that your child will be overjoyed to do their homework alone in their room. If they have homework, ask them if they would like any help with it. If they want to do it alone, bring them healthy snacks and give them a break after each hour of work. This will help them keep their mind active and focused as they concentrate on any given task.

Homework Enjoyment

By encouraging homework and making it fun, you can also improve how your child behaves in their day-to-day life. Homework can be a very stressful experience, especially when a child is having difficulty with the material. Even if you're having trouble understanding what your child was assigned to do, make the most of it. By making it fun and exciting and getting yourself involved, you'll be able to ensure that future homework assignments are an opportunity for you to spend time together and help your child succeed at school.

REMEMBER:

- *Even after making homework fun, it still may be a struggle for your child.*
- *Do your best to help your child and only arrange for a tutor as a last resort.*
- *Let them know that once homework is complete, they have all the free time they want before bed.*

Counselor Connection
connecting parent-child-school

Improving Your Child's Unique Study Skills

Solid study skills are crucial for developing children, even though studying in their early years may not be as important as it will become in the future. However, with this in mind, it's always essential to consider that each child has a unique way of dealing with work. You can encourage a child to develop their own types of study skills by actively participating in the process, and encouraging them to strive for better grades no matter how old they are.

Benefits of Establishing Study Skills Early

As a parent, strive to establish these study skills while your child is still very young. With repetition and time, they will eventually take on the necessary skills you're trying to instill. For example, a first-grade math test may not seem like a big deal to you or your child, but by sitting with them (just like you would over homework), you'll be able to walk them through how to approach a subject with confidence and ease. Confidence is a major part of any young child's development of good study skills. When children are unsure of themselves while they are working, they may be more than likely to discard the study habits you've been working toward developing with them.

Communicate with Educators

Talking with teachers and getting a good sense for how your child behaves in class (i.e., how they approach their work and how enthusiastic they are about the content covered) is also a very necessary step any parent can take. To get a good feel for how you should approach studying at home, talk to teachers about how the content is being taught in school. If your child is struggling in math or English, for example, ask those teachers for suggestions on additional study material. You can make the material fun and enjoyable by creating something your child will actually like, including interactive work or work that allows them to employ their creativity while still absorbing the content.

REMEMBER:

- *Is your child naturally adept at the content? Can you make it fun and creative for them?*
- *Encouraging study time and making it an event that your child looks forward to will shape how they approach it in the future.*
- *Practicing outside of study time may also be necessary, and can make your child feel confident and smart.*

Counselor Connection

connecting parent-child-school

Increasing a Child's Likelihood to Respect Differences

There is an increasing amount of diversity within school systems these days. Throughout their young lives, children will be exposed to many different types of people and cultures. Their reactions to these different individuals will be primarily based on how you behave in similar situations; at a young age, many children do not consider skin color to be a difference between people. However, your influence is stronger than you think. By controlling your own personal biases in these types of situations, you can teach your child the necessary steps toward respecting and honoring differences among others.

Be Receptive to Discussion

In many circumstances, racism doesn't come into play at a young age. The only noticeable behavior among children when they're pointing out differences from themselves is a physical handicap or something they can see is very different. By opening a line of communication and talking about how to respect others in a healthy way, you can encourage your child to respect and honor differences. Reflect on how you behave around people who are different — you'd be surprised at how children pick up on your social cues. Because you behave a certain way around someone, they may pick up those similar behaviors so always be conscious of modeling the behaviors and attitudes you would like to see in your children.

Be Open and Up-front

Acknowledging people's differences in a simple and clear way is also important. If a child asks you about someone's skin color or why they are in a wheelchair, be as honest and simple as possible. When a child asks a question about someone, they are expecting an immediate and understandable answer. Teaching them what sets people apart is important, but reminding them that everyone is human and deserves to be respected is even more important.

REMEMBER:

- *Ultimately, the way you react around different people will affect how your child does the same.*
- *Encourage your child to tell teachers about bullying circumstances involving children who are different, whether that's race, language or ability.*
- *Remind your child that while people may be physically different, everyone is really the same and should be treated as such.*

connecting parent-child-school

Increasing Parental Involvement in School

Students with involved parents tend to do better in school than their classmates whose parents are not involved at their school. When parents are involved in their children's schools, they're helping show their children that they value education.

Parental Involvement is Key

Unfortunately, when there are discipline problems at school or if children are having a hard time learning a subject, all too often the blame is placed on the teacher. While teachers should be in control of their classrooms, children need involved parents to help teach them discipline at home. Parents can help their children learn better in school by helping them with their homework. Parents who take the time to get involved with their children's education are showing how much they value education and care about their children doing well in school.

However, helping with homework or disciplining children at home for misbehaving in school is just a starting point. Parents also need to be more involved with school activities to help support their children and demonstrate that what is important for their children is important to them as well. Children will learn that they're valued if their parents are involved in what they do.

Ways for Parents to Get Involved

There are many things a parent can do to be involved in their children's education. One of the most important ways a parent can be involved is to show up for parent-teacher conferences and school events, such as an open house or science fair.

Getting involved inside the classroom as volunteers is another good way for parents to participate in their children's education. They can help teachers with handouts, be available to help children with problems they're having with a school subject, and just be a positive presence in the classroom. Parents can also volunteer to help with after-school activities as well — especially if they can't leave work to be in the classroom during the day. Help organize a bake sale, usher at a school play, or help coach children during after-school sports. There are many ways parents can be involved at school.

REMEMBER:

- *Children with involved parents often do better in school.*
- *Parents getting involved at school show their children how to value education.*
- *Parents getting involved shows their children how much they're valued.*

Counselor Connection

connecting parent-child-school

Instilling Manners in Children

Teaching good manners is a way to help children connect with other people — especially people they may have just met. It may take some time to instill good manners in children, but with perseverance, it can be done.

Why Do Children Need to Learn Good Manners?

Children need to learn good manners from an early age so they'll repeat them throughout their lives and to get along with other people, whether they're strangers, parents, or extended family members. Having good manners will make your child stand out in a crowd because, unfortunately, teaching good behavior seems to be a thing of the past. When children demonstrate good manners, they are also demonstrating respect for the people around them.

While a five-year-old may not need to make a good impression, having good manners will get positive attention from people, helping to reinforce the manners they are learning. As they get older, when they do need to make good impressions on people, their good manners will shine through and people will remember them for their politeness. Whether it's at school, at church, or meeting a friend's parents, demonstrating good manners will make a lasting impression.

What Manners Should Children Learn?

There are many manners children can start learning from the time they learn how to speak. Most of these manners will be verbal, such as saying the following:
- Please
- Thank You
- Excuse Me
- No Thank You
- Yes Sir/Ma'am
- No Sir/Ma'am

While many of these sayings seem to be old fashioned, they demonstrate good behavior. One of the best ways for children to learn these manners are for their parents to demonstrate them in front of their children. Whenever they get anything from a restaurant or from a friend, saying "Please" and "Thank You" will be remembered by children.

Another manner children should learn from an early age is to send a thank you note whenever they receive a gift, whether it was from a friend or a grandparent. They should also never use foul language, refrain from using potty humor in front of others, and cover their mouths or noses with an elbow when they cough or sneeze. These are just a few manners young children should learn.

REMEMBER:

- *Demonstrate manners children should learn.*
- *Reinforce good manners with praise.*
- *Teach children appropriate public behavior.*

Counselor Connection

connecting parent-child-school

Instilling Perseverance in Children

It's easy for a child to give up on a task that seems too difficult. However, encouraging your child to persevere to accomplish a task is a great way to build their self-confidence, as well as show how rewarding it can be to overcome difficulties and accomplish something they thought they couldn't.

Why Teaching Perseverance is Important

If children are permitted to just give up on a task they think is too hard, they may eventually develop a fear of trying to overcome obstacles in their lives or of trying new things. However, by being persistent when they're trying to learn a new subject in school or a new task, children will learn the value of hard work and how good it feels when they accomplish something they consider difficult.

Being persistent can also help children develop self-confidence. When they do persevere and accomplish something, children need to have their perseverance reinforced with praise from both their teachers and parents. For small children, learning to tie their shoes can be difficult, but if they persevere, they'll master tying their shoes and move on to learn the next new skill. Praise children for their efforts and accomplishments to help build their self-esteem and confidence.

How to Teach Perseverance

Children usually learn from their parents by watching and imitating their behavior. If their parents give up on difficult tasks easily, children will learn that behavior as well. However, parents can model perseverance by continuing to make an effort to learn new skills, overcome difficulties, and accomplish their goals. When their parents are rewarded with a promotion and/or pay raise, children will learn there can be rewards for persevering on a task.

Parents can also use language to help children make the connection between their hard work and success. For instance, rather than just giving general praise, tell them that their practice has paid off — that playing their instrument, their grade in math class, or their sports performance has gotten much better. Make the direct connection between their perseverance and their accomplishments. Not only will they learn to persevere, but they can learn self-discipline as well.

REMEMBER:

- *Adults need to model perseverance for children.*
- *Praise children by connecting their accomplishments with their hard work.*
- *Teaching children perseverance will help them build confidence, boost self-esteem, and learn self-discipline.*

connecting parent-child-school

How to Teach Your Child About Diversity in Others

Diversity can be a difficult subject to approach for many parents. Because the topic is often uncomfortable, many parents choose to ignore it completely and let their children come to their opinions and attitudes on their own. It is much better for parents or guardian to leverage the direct influence they have over a child's developing behavior to shape their opinions and attitudes in the right direction. Children can and nearly always do pick up behaviors not only from you, but from those around them at school. Illustrating exactly what makes people diverse and how to approach others who see diversity negatively is an important moral lesson that your child will take with them through the rest of their life.

How Children See Others

Children are naturally drawn to one another, no matter their differences. At a very young age, they may not question why someone has a different skin color or speaks in a different way, whether that is because of a speech impediment or a different native language. However, expect the conversation to come up at some point— and be prepared for it. Just because you think your child treats everyone equally no matter what they look or sound like doesn't mean they don't have questions about it. When they ask you about differences, they aren't being critical – just observant and curious. You should be excited when your child approaches you with this conversation before you have to bring it up.

Using Books to Demonstrate Diversity

There are many books and resources geared toward teaching children about diversity. Whether nonfiction or fiction, these books can help them understand why everyone can be different while still being equal. Sitting with your child and helping them understand the messages in these material, along with answering any questions they have about specific instances of diversity, can shed some much-needed light and give them guidance for the future. Establishing the importance of diversity at a young age is essential for helping children forge lasting bonds with all types of people.

REMEMBER:

- *Children often pick up habits from you, so model respect of diversity in your own life.*
- *Ask your child if they have any questions about certain topics regarding diversity.*
- *No matter what they say, their mind is innocent. Children are both observant and curious!*

Counselor Connection

connecting parent-child-school

Motivating Children

Motivating children to do things they don't want to do can be difficult, but you can help them learn self-motivation by showing them the rewards for their accomplishments. These rewards don't have to be gifts or prizes, but children can learn to accomplish tasks for the sense of pride these rewards can bring.

The Barriers to Motivation

If children don't seem motivated to learn new tasks or schoolwork, there may be barriers they're not discussing with anyone. Children who don't read or write well may be too embarrassed to admit their difficulties — especially when facing criticism in school or at home, despite trying to do their best. This can often lead to outward signs of frustration, such as anger or misbehaving in school.

Other motivation barriers may exist at home. If parents seem to not care about whether their children are doing well at school or if they don't follow through on promises they make to their children, then kids may not care about learning or trying to accomplish tasks at home. Children often take their cues from the adults in their lives, so if the adults don't seem to care what happens with their children, why should the children care?

Ways to Motivate Children

There are many positive ways to motivate children in both the classroom and at home. Refrain from using punishment as a motivator. This can lead children to learn to resent the task their teacher or parents are trying to get them to accomplish. While punishment may work for a while, it can make children so frustrated over time that they lash out when they're having a hard time accomplishing tasks or learning difficult subjects.

Take the time to find out why your child doesn't feel motivated to learn something or try a new skill. It could be that they are afraid of being laughed at if they fail, or that they may be having difficulty reading, writing, or using another skill in class that their friends have an easy time with. Talk to your child about their lack of motivation to find out the real reason behind it.

REMEMBER:

- *Don't assume you know what's causing a lack of motivation. Talk to them about it.*
- *Show interest in what children are doing. This can motivate them to do their best.*
- *Refrain from using punishment to motivate children.*

connecting parent-child-school

Overcoming School Phobias

School phobias are a very real concern for children of all ages. If your child is pretending to be sick, begging not to go to school, or is otherwise anxious about entering the school halls, perhaps it's not simply a lack of motivation. School phobias affect approximately 3-9% of all children in kindergarten through eighth grade. This could be one of the causes of your child's school-related troubles.

A Look at School Phobias

A school phobia is something that makes a child uneasy about going to school. There are various levels of phobia, and for some children they can become so severe that they become physically ill from the simple thought of getting on the bus in the morning.

Interestingly, however, students with phobias also typically have a higher level of intelligence than their peers. Phobias usually exist when there is also another underlying medical condition, such as ADD or ADHD. If your child refuses to go to school or you have a battle on your hands five days a week, it is a good idea to take your child to your pediatrician. The doctor can perform an evaluation and recommend treatment if it is warranted.

Are There Symptoms?

There are noticeable symptoms with school phobias. As mentioned above, students can become severely ill because they're so upset about going to school.

They could develop vomiting, nausea and diarrhea. In some severe cases, it's even possible for a child to pass out or faint.

There are a number of causes of school phobias. Something such as changes within the family, stress at home, or even bullying can be causing the phobia.

There is good news is that most school phobias are typically not long-term conditions. They usually subside within a few weeks. It might feel like it's a lot longer when you're in the middle of it!

REMEMBER:

- *Try to talk to your child and understand what's causing their resistance to school. Be patient and understanding — avoid blaming or accusing them.*
- *Ask lots of questions — especially if your child's phobia of going to school is recent.*
- *Talk to the school, including teachers, guidance counselors, and the principal. Having an open line of communication can help you discover things you might otherwise miss. This can make a world of difference in solving the issue.*

Counselor Connection

connecting parent-child-school

Perfectionism in Children

Perfection is something that many children strive for, usually without an understanding that no one is perfect. These types of children go to great lengths to be perfect — to make all the right moves and decisions in life. It can be very detrimental to a child who's unable to accomplish a goal that, in itself, would be impossible for anyone to accomplish.

A Look at Perfectionism

Children who are perfectionists want to do tasks that sometimes are out of their reach. They have very high standards for themselves, and find it frustrating when unable to achieve goals they've set even when it's clear to everyone else they're obviously overreaching themselves. Signs of perfectionism include the following:

- Being very critical of themselves or embarrassed over small things.
- Having anxiety when something doesn't go as expected.
- Is very sensitive to criticism from others.
- Is very critical of others.
- Exhibits headaches, vomiting, nausea or other symptoms when something goes wrong.

There are a number of causes of the condition. It can be anything from unrealistic expectations and pressure from parents to factors in the outside world.

How to Help a Child with Perfectionism

As a parent, you want to help your child be the best they can be, so what are you to do when it seems that everything you've instilled in your child is coming back to haunt you? It can be difficult to deal with perfectionism in a child, but it's very much something you can help them control.

REMEMBER:

- *Let your children know that no one on Earth is perfect. We all make mistakes, and it's from those mistakes that we're able to learn and do better in the future.*
- *Don't be critical of your child and their behaviors. Be positive, and encourage them as often as possible.*
- *Admit that you make mistakes. When you make them, point them out to your child — but make sure to do so in a non-critical manner.*
- *Don't compare your child to others.*
- *Get involved with your child's school. Talk to their teachers and inform them of what's going on. More can be accomplished together than alone.*
- *Help your child understand that what they are trying to achieve is impossible for both them and anyone else who tries to be perfect.*

connecting parent-child-school

The Responsibility a Child Has to Play Fairly

Learning to play fairly with others is often a difficult task for children. When it comes to children who are in preschool or in daycare facilities, the concept of sharing is taught to them in various ways. However, as a parent, you can also help teach them how important it is to share with and be kind to their peers and family. By following a few helpful tips, you'll be able to ensure your child plays fairly with and shares with others.

Promoting Sharing Habits in the Home

If your child has siblings, many toys will become the object of competition. The winner will get to play with the toy in the end, leaving the other child to cry and fuss. If this becomes a persistent scenario, start intervening and taking the toy away from the dominant child with a simple statement that it's the other child's turn. That way, you're teaching your child about sharing without directly communicating about it. Actions will speak more loudly than words most of the time, so you need to exhibit the behaviors you want to see in your children first. Combining actions with words provides the best opportunity for teaching sharing behaviors.

Encouraging Your Child to Share with Other Children at School

If your child has a favorite toy they like to play with or activity they like to participate in at school, try and find out if they are actively sharing and letting other people join in on the fun. Talking to children about the benefits of sharing (how fun it can be, how they can make new friends and have new experiences, etc.) may encourage them to share on their own. Talk to teachers if your child's sharing habits at home have you concerned about what might be happening at school.

REMEMBER:

- *When your child isn't playing fairly with you or a sibling at home, take action immediately.*
- *Help your child come to understand that sharing and playing fairly can be much more fun than playing alone.*
- *Share with your child, and they will share with you as well, and then be more likely to share with others.*

Counselor Connection
connecting parent-child-school

The Troubles with Friendship Triangles

Children go through many sets of friendships as they grow. Some will flourish and some will fizzle out. You can't control how these relationships will play out since they're your child's own experiences, but you must understand that sometimes it's important to intervene. Friendship triangles can be a fun-but-sometimes-difficult dynamic. In these circumstances, when you consider how important it is for your child to develop healthy relationships at this fragile age, you'll be able to make a practical evaluation of your child's relationships and intervene when it becomes necessary.

The Triangle

A friendship triangle can lead to bullying — and nobody wants to have their child suffer through any sort of bullying experience. For example, let's say your child has two friends. The three of them hang out all the time, both in and outside of school. Suddenly, your child does something that upsets one of the friends. The dynamic of fun and friendly play can turn quickly and suddenly into every parent's worst nightmare. The antagonism that blossoms can spread like a disease; the moment two friends have made an alliance against the third, the previously happy threesome might never be the same again.

Communicating with your child and stressing the importance of branching out with friends as opposed to staying sheltered with just two could help them greatly if this type of situation arises. Even though you can't always have a direct impact on what happens with your child's relationships, gently encouraging them to branch out socially is always a good idea.

Helping Your Child

If your child feels alienated or stressed from a friendship-triangle squabble, it's important for you to remember that you can't become frustrated with their decisions. You're in a role where your child will turn to you for solace and comfort, which is exactly what you should offer. Just because they said or did something in their friendship triangle that hurt someone doesn't mean you should criticize or scold them for it. After all, everyone makes mistakes.

REMEMBER:

- *Encouraging your child to always be social is very important.*
- *Try talking with parents if any issues arise that affect relationships between your child and theirs.*
- *Be an olive branch for your child, giving them comfort and solace in difficult situations.*

Counselor Connection
connecting parent-child-school

Understanding Self-Esteem

While most people associate self-esteem issues with older children, young children can also suffer from low self-esteem. These children need help from both their schools and parents to build up their self-esteem so they can be happy with themselves.

Understanding Low Self-Esteem

Self-esteem is how one feels about oneself, and how that person judges their own self-worth. In young children, low self-esteem can be caused by a variety of factors, including how others treat them. Usually, low self-esteem isn't a natural state — especially in young children. Some of the behaviors demonstrated by others that can affect children's self-esteem include the following:

- Being bullied by classmates at school.
- Being told by teachers that they're not very smart.
- Having parents yell at them and/or criticizing them constantly.
- Negative self-talk, usually brought on by others' criticisms.

If a child has parents with low self-esteem, they may also develop low self-esteem — especially if the parents are constantly criticizing them, yelling at them, or using harsh words with them. Low self-esteem may also develop because a child thinks they are inferior to others due to how they look or their lack of money, education or nice things like the right clothes.

How to Help Build Self-Esteem

Demonstrate love for a child by praising them for their good behavior or accomplishments in school. Even if they were not as successful as you would've liked, praise them for giving their best effort. This will also teach your child how to persevere when faced with challenges in school, at home, or with friends. If children do need criticism for behavior or for something that happened at school, give constructive criticism in a calm manner.

Encourage children to develop their talents by praising their efforts in something they love. If your child likes to paint or draw, or if they play sports or perform music, praise them when they do well. Even further, participate in the activity with your child to show your interest in what they are doing.

Knowing that a parent cares about a child's hobby or talent will go a long way in helping a child develop better self-esteem. Support their efforts in a positive, affirming manner. You can also build a child's confidence by allowing them to pick out what they wear, develop their friendships, and have a voice in family decisions.

REMEMBER:

- *Praise children for doing well in school and/or at home.*
- *If criticism is needed, make it constructive so they can learn from mistakes.*
- *Be involved with your children in their activities and hobbies.*

Counselor Connection

connecting parent-child-school

When is it Okay for Children to Tattle?

Children of many different backgrounds will go through the same developmental woes that parents dread. Tattling is one of these woes. Even though it can be used for good (e.g., when a child is reporting a bully, sees something that isn't right), tattling can also be used in negative ways. If you respond too much to a child's tattling on others (particularly their siblings or friends), they may lose a lot of respect and friendship from these people. You have to actively encourage your child to be honest, but not to push boundaries with others.

Why Children Tattle

Most of the time, it's healthy for children to tattle. If a child sees their siblings doing something they aren't allowed to do and tell you, they shouldn't be rewarded for it. You'll be encouraging a behavior that may turn out either good or bad — it all depends on the child, and how often they tattle. In good circumstances, when a child tattles, it's not too often and it's always about something important. If you're too receptive or thankful when your child tattles to you, however, it may become a habit that not everyone else will appreciate. Especially when it comes to relationships between your child and their friends at school, if tattling (i.e., seeking out attention and rewards from adults) becomes persistent, they could become a target for bullying.

Discussing Tattling

Explaining to your child that there are appropriate and inappropriate times to tattle is crucial in helping them understand the difference between right and wrong. Encourage them to tell you things at home that they see are wrong, but wrong in the way that it doesn't feel right – not just because they don't like the way their sibling is behaving. Explain to your child that if they went around tattling on everyone at school for everything they did, some people will probably get angry about it. Let them know it's always good to be honest, but it's not their place to inform on everyone for every little thing that happens.

REMEMBER:

- *Children will often tattle to seek attention.*
- *Tattling is a natural habit that can be curbed with age and persistence.*
- *Reevaluate how you've interacted with your child that day, and make adjustments yourself if you might inadvertently be encouraging excessive tattling.*

connecting parent-child-school

When Teasing Turns into Bullying

Bullying is a major problem in many schools around the world. It has been around for years, and is often a very difficult problem for teachers and parents to solve. Teasing can be a very natural part of any child's experience at school, whether they are on the giving or receiving end. If you find out that your child is teasing other kinds at school, there are steps you can take to make sure it doesn't turn into something more serious. By addressing the teasing head on, you can help your child see the error of their ways and prevent these behaviors in the future.

Teasing at Home

Many children tease their siblings or others at home as a result of some sort of peer pressure. This is more applicable in a school setting, where a child will want to fit in and, to do so, will point out differences in someone else to put them down. Even the gentlest teasing can hurt another child in ways you couldn't imagine. If your household is often filled with both you, your spouse, and your other children/family members teasing one another, this behavior may not translate well outside the home. Be careful about the types of language and behavior your child could pick up at home.

Behind the Teasing

Children also tease others to gain attention or deal with stress they feel in other parts of their lives. By consulting with teachers and other adults who are involved with your child during the day, you'll be able to get an accurate assessment of what's really going on. Just because you don't think there are problems at home doesn't mean there isn't an underlying factor you haven't considered. Be open and questioning about yourself when you learn that your child's teasing has somehow led to bullying.

REMEMBER:

- *Talk to your child about their teasing habits at home and/or school. Explain gently but firmly that this is not okay.*
- *Discourage teasing at home with other family members, including yourself.*
- *Remember that peer pressure from other children may play a part.*

Counselor Connection
connecting parent-child-school

When Worry Affects Your Child

When negative emotion is affecting your child, you'll be able to tell through a series of behaviors or mannerisms displayed. In order to sway your child from being overly worried and letting that worry translate into their daily life, you need to consider a variety of different factors that may have lead to the initial trigger. By talking with your child and helping them understand that you are always there to help, you'll create a safe and friendly environment where they feel they can express their worries, no matter what they are.

Childhood Stress vs. Adulthood Stress

When worry affects a child, it's a very different situation from when it affects an adult. Worry can translate into your child shutting down or behaving in a way that you're not used to. Although it may be a shock at first, you always have to remember that just because your child appears to have changed drastically doesn't mean they're a completely different person now. Sometimes, tragedy, bullying, or loss – or even your own problems at home – can bring out a great deal of anxiety and worry in your child. As a parent, you can help them understand these feelings and talk over anything you can do to help curb their stress.

Lasting Effects of Stress

When it comes to worry in a child, the effects, if left untreated, can carry on or be buried within them for years. If your child doesn't know how to deal with stress or doesn't understand that they can turn to you in times of need, they may be more likely in the future to let worry build up until it explodes as aggression or another type of negative emotion or behavior. You must maintain a dialogue when you sense your child is troubled, no matter how hard it may be even for you at the time. It's important not to be selfish in situations that affect a whole family, which cause worry. Children are more impacted in the long term than you are.

REMEMBER:

- *Make sure your child knows you're always there to talk.*
- *Help your child understand that worries fade away in time, and friends and family are there to help them through their tough feelings.*
- *Give your child some personal space, but not too much. Always be there for them.*

Counselor Connection

connecting parent-child-school

Teaching Children How to Follow Directions and Listen Effectively

Many children in their developmental stages will shy away from following directions and listening. It's a natural reaction; children don't want to be told what to do, because the world is so fresh and new. However, it's important that, as a parent, you understand the necessity for developing these skills at an early age. If your child chooses not to listen to your directions, they may do the same in school and continue to do so for the rest of their life. By instilling a sense of importance and urgency around following directions and listening effectively, you can help your child come to understand why it's so important to you and the rest of the family.

When a Child Doesn't Listen, Employ Defensive Strategies

Let's say your child throws a tantrum in the middle of the grocery store and won't stop screaming. As a parent, would you leave the store with your child immediately, or give them what they want? Many parents would choose the latter simply to make their child be quiet. This is not the optimal choice for teaching children how to listen and follow directions in the long run! Gentle but firm is the prescription for these situations.

Just because you think it's okay this one time, it isn't — your child will automatically resort to crying and fits to get what they want from that point forward. It is far better to experience the momentary discomfort than set this pattern up for future repetition.

Listening Is Just as Important as Following Directions

Helping your child become a better listener is the second step. When you tell them to do something and they give you an attitude, have them repeat your first direction. If they still refuse to listen, you might have to resort to disciplinary action.

REMEMBER:

- *Never respond to your child's request just because it's for something they wants. Do they deserve it? Why or why not?*
- *Rely on other members of your family to help with these steps, and illustrate the need for everyone to help out. When it comes from everyone, your child will likely change their ways.*
- *Encourage your child to be open with you in a healthy way, no matter how old they are.*

Counselor Connection

connecting parent-child-school

Teaching Your Child the Importance of Personal Space

Personal space is important for any individual. Children, however, often don't have an understanding of the concept, or how uncomfortable people can become when their personal space is "invaded." As a parent, you can teach them how to respect the personal space of their peers, family members, and other adults in their lives. By stressing the importance of a personal bubble and encouraging a child to respect the space of everyone around them, you'll be able to ensure they avoid conflict in difficult situations where people feel their personal space is being violated.

Creating a Personal Bubble around Yourself

When a child lacks respect for personal space in the middle of a task, employ the "bubble theory." This means you put up an invisible bubble of a certain size around yourself, and ask your child to respect that space. If your child disagrees at first, make the space farther and farther away. If they continue to resist, send them to their room or use another method of discipline. After a few repeated efforts of this, begin to offer your child small rewards if they respect your space when you ask. A code word when they are becoming too close to others is also important; something familiar, like "personal bubble," will help your child remember the need for people's personal space.

Rewarding a Child for Continually Respecting Others' Space

If you go a long period of time without having to tell your child when to respect the space of others, it's likely that the message has sunk in enough to become habitual. Reward them for having remembered this behavior, and encourage them to continue practicing it as much as possible while reminding your child that hugs and kisses are still okay.

REMEMBER:

- *The "bubble theory" is a good idea for younger children who always demand attention.*
- *Children will not always want to be cuddled, but may feel anxiety or loneliness. In these circumstances, you'll likely be able to tell which is which and make the right decision on your response.*
- *By giving children a small-yet-reasonable distance to respect, they'll feel more comfortable.*

connecting parent-child-school

Ten Ways to Involve Fathers in Their Children's Education

Having both parents involved in their children's education is vital to the child's success. If the parents are divorced, the parents and school should make an extra effort to include the father in the child's education instead of leaving it all up to the mother or other custodial parent.

How the School Can Keep Fathers Informed

There are many ways the school can act to keep fathers involved in their children's education — especially if the parents are divorced and the mother is the custodial parent. They can:

Make sure that progress information about the child goes out to both parents.

Invite both parents to school events, such as parent-teacher conferences, science fairs, and other academic events in which the child is involved.

Have a "Bring Your Dad to School Day." Make it an event, and encourage all fathers to attend. Have a special luncheon, or another way to recognize the fathers' efforts for attending the event.

Encourage fathers to help their children with their homework assignments, such as checking them over before they're turned in to the teachers.

Welcome fathers to meet their children's teachers. Have teachers collect fathers' information (phone numbers, addresses, etc.) if different from the mothers'.

How Fathers Can Keep Themselves Involved

Volunteer to be a sports coach, set designer for a play, or usher for special events. By doing this, you'll help your child see that you feel that their activities are important.

Take children to the library and encourage them to read rather than play video games or watch TV.

Model the types of behaviors that students need, such as politeness, getting their work done on time, and sharing their belongings with others.

Have family mealtimes. Discuss how the day went and encourage your child to talk about their day at school.

Take time to let your child know how much you enjoy spending time with them, even at school functions.

REMEMBER:

- *Keep single fathers in the loop regarding their children's education.*
- *Volunteer for school events, whether they're related to academia, entertainment, or sports.*
- *Make an effort to invite fathers to parent-teacher conferences and other school functions.*
- *Tell children that time with them is special to their fathers.*

Counselor Connection

connecting parent-child-school

The Essential Skill of Self-Control

All children need to be taught self-control, along with the consequences of their actions if they don't restrain their own desires, impulses, or emotions. Taking a moment to pause and consider their actions is a learned behavior that will help children throughout their lives.

Why Self-Control Is Important

Learning how to control one's own impulses allows children to get along better with their classmates, teachers, and parents. Self-control is a skill that will follow children throughout their lives, helping them get along with others and not do the first thing that pops into their heads. Without exhibiting self-control, adults often end up in trouble, or even in jail.

Helping children learn self-discipline by encouraging their good behaviors can also help them learn self-control. Set limits to help them learn self-discipline, such as having a set bedtime and sticking with it. If parents and teachers demonstrate consistency with what they ask children to do, there will be less frustration, because children will know what's expected of them. Without these expectations, children may not learn self-control skills.

How to Teach Children Self-Control

Self-control is a behavior most children can be taught. There are children who can't learn this behavior due to disabilities, but most kids do well when they're taught how to take a moment to think about their actions before reacting to a situation. The best way to teach this behavior is to model it for children.

When a teacher, parent, or other adult becomes frustrated or angry, he or she needs to take a moment before reacting. Instead of yelling, using harsh language, or even physically reacting to a situation, if an adult can show self-control when in a super-charged emotional state, this subsequently demonstrates to children how to react appropriately to volatile situations.

If a teacher or parent sees a situation in which a child may jump to react to something verbally or physically, he or she can help that child by teaching them to breathe deeply and inwardly consider the consequences of their reactions to a situation. Getting children involved with activities that teach self-discipline is also a good way to teach self-control.

REMEMBER:

- *Model self-control in front of your children.*
- *Set limits and expectations for children to learn self-control.*
- *Have children get involved with activities that involve self-discipline.*

ABOUT THE AUTHOR |
Erainna Winnett, Ed. S.

Erainna was born and raised in central Louisiana. The oldest of five children she always yearned to be a teacher and forced her siblings to play school year round. Naturally, she graduated with a teaching degree in 1995 and earned her Master's degree in 2000. Five years later she earned her Education Specialist degree in early childhood education. After fifteen years in the classroom, she moved to the role of school counselor and has never been happier.

While serving as school counselor at an elementary school in northeast Texas, she frequently uses children's books as therapy to help her students heal, learn, and grow. Ideas for her books come from the students she works with on a daily basis. Her goal, as an author, is to touch the hearts of children, one story at a time. Erainna lives on a 300 acre cattle ranch near the Red River with her husband, two daughters, three dogs, two horses, and one ill-tempered cat.

To see more books by Erainna, please visit her counseling website counselingwithheart.com.

Notes: